At Night

By Liza Charlesworth

ISBN: 978-1-339-02783-8

Art Director: Tannaz Fassihi; Designer: Tanya Chernyak
Photos © Getty Images and Shutterstock.com.
Copyright © Liza Charlesworth. All rights reserved. Published by Scholastic Inc.

1 2 3 4 5 6 7 8 9 10   68   32 31 30 29 28 27 26 25 24 23

Printed in Jiaxing, China. First printing, August 2023.

At night, it is not light.
It is not bright.
But you might see
a lot of sights.

You might see a deer at night.
It eats twigs and green grass.
That is quite a sight!

You might spot a moth.
It has white and pink wings.
It flies up so high!

If you are right by a pond,
you might spot a big frog.
"Croak, croak!" it cries.

Might you see a fox? Yes!
It runs and it slinks.
It tries to hide in the trees.

close-up

Flap, flap, zip, zap!
You might see a bunch of bugs.
Their bright tails light up.

close-up

At night, you might see
1000 bats take flight.
But do not feel fright.
It is a fine sight!